INVESTIGATING A CRIME SCENE

Follow the Clues

by Tamra B. Orr

CHERRY LAKE PUBLISHING · ANN ARBOR, MICHIGAN

Published in the United States of America by Cherry Lake Publishing
Ann Arbor, Michigan
www.cherrylakepublishing.com

CONTENT EDITOR: Robert Wolffe, EdD, Professor of Teacher Education, Bradley University, Peoria, Illinois
BOOK DESIGN AND ILLUSTRATION: The Design Lab
READING ADVISER: Marla Conn, ReadAbility, Inc.

PHOTO CREDITS: Cover and page 1, ©Ammentorp Photography/Shutterstock, Inc.; page 4, ©razihusin/
Shutterstock, Inc.; page 5, ©Jochen Tack/Alamy; page 6, ©Eddie Gerald/Alamy; page 8, ©Shi Yali/
Shutterstock, Inc.; page 9, ©By Ian Miles-Flashpoint Pictures/Alamy; page 10, © jcjgphotography/
Shutterstock, Inc.; page 12, ©Mikael Karlsson/Alamy; page 13, ©bikeriderlondon/Shutterstock, Inc.; page
14, ©Gladskikh Tatiana/Shutterstock, Inc.; page 15, ©Diego Cervo/Shutterstock, Inc.; page 16, ©Leah-Anne
Thompson/Shutterstock; page 17, ©Paul Matzner/Alamy; page 18, ©Georgios Kollidas/Shutterstock, Inc.;
page 19, ©You Touch Pix of EuToch/Shutterstock, Inc.; page 20, ©Justek16/Shutterstock, Inc.; page 21,
©Africa Studio/Shutterstock, Inc.; page 22, ©maradonna 8888/Shutterstock, Inc.; page 23, Photo by baughj
/ http://www.flickr.com / CC BY-SA 2.0; page 24, ©Peter Kim/Shutterstock, Inc.; page 25, ©iStockphoto.
com/stray_cat; pages 26 and 27, ©Monkey Business Images/Shutterstock, Inc.; page 28, ©Fisun Ivan/
Shutterstock, Inc.

LIBRARY OF CONGRESS CATALOGING-IN-PUBLICATION DATA
Orr, Tamra, author.
    Investigating a crime scene / by Tamra B. Orr.
        pages cm. — (Science explorer) (Follow the clues)
    Summary: "Use the scientific method to learn how crime scene investigators gather
evidence to solve crimes."—Provided by publisher.
    Audience: Grade 4 to 6.
    ISBN 978-1-62431-777-4 (lib. bdg.) — ISBN 978-1-62431-787-3 (pbk.) —
ISBN 978-1-62431-807-8 (e-book) —ISBN 978-1-62431-797-2 (pdf)
    1. Criminal investigation—Juvenile literature. 2. Crime scene searches—Juvenile
literature. 3. Forensic sciences—Juvenile literature. I. Title. II. Series: Science explorer.

        HV8073.8.O774 2014
        363.25—dc23   2013036996

Cherry Lake Publishing would like to acknowledge the work of The Partnership for 21st Century Skills.
Please visit www.p21.org for more information.

Printed in the United States of America, Corporate Graphics Inc.
January 2014

TABLE OF CONTENTS

CHAPTER 1

FINDING THE CRIME

Jonathan was so excited to start the day that he awoke before his alarm clock went off.

Jonathan's eyes flew open before the alarm could ring. He had been looking forward to this day too long to risk oversleeping. Today he was not going to school. He was going to work with his father. His homework assignment was to shadow his dad at work and learn about what he did, and then write a report about it. Jonathan's father was a professional sketch preparer for the police department. Jonathan thought it was the coolest job.

Jonathan had told Mrs. Coffman, his teacher, that a sketch preparer diagrammed, or drew, a crime scene. Jonathan's dad, Mr. Elliot, rode along with police officers to the location of the crime. Once there, he took careful measurements of all the evidence. He double-checked his work to make sure everything was correct, because police officers, and possibly lawyers, would use his drawings.

His detailed sketches showed the location and relationship of all objects and any evidence, such as blood spatters, footprints, and broken glass. The investigation team's photographer took pictures of the crime scene. Other investigators made notes about what they observed.

While investigating a car crash, a sketch preparer might draw a diagram showing which direction the vehicles were going in when they collided.

Police stations are busy places, full of people coming and going.

Walking into the police station never lost its thrill for Jonathan.

"Ed!" someone shouted to Mr. Elliot. "The community bicycle center was broken into this morning. We need to get out there quickly."

Jonathan frowned. The center was one of his favorite places in town. Who would want to damage it? Hopefully, his dad would help figure out the answer.

"Let's head out to the truck, Jon," said Mr. Elliot. He handed his son a dark blue police vest. "You're a member of our team today, so you have to look the part.

"Let's go! Pencils locked and loaded," Mr. Elliot said, grinning.

It was time to go to a crime scene.

PART OF THE TEAM

No crime is ever solved by a single person. Instead it takes a skillful team working together to follow the clues, analyze them, and figure out who may have committed a crime. Along with the sketcher, the members of most investigative teams include:

- ☆ a team leader
- ☆ a photographer
- ☆ an evidence recorder
- ☆ various specialists

The *leader* takes control of the team, making sure all members do their jobs and have the supplies and materials they need. *Photographers* take pictures of the crime scene area, including people, vehicles, and the surrounding area as well. Some of their photographs will reveal **impression evidence**, such as prints left behind by feet, vehicle tires, or tools. Photographers log all of this in a special journal. *Evidence recorders* are like crime custodians. They put on gloves to bag evidence, and then label, sign, and date the bags. They do this to make sure evidence is not damaged or lost and is given to the right people to maintain **chain of custody**. For certain crimes, a variety of *specialists* who have additional knowledge in important areas are brought in, including:

- ☆ **surveyors**
- ☆ bomb technicians
- ☆ medical examiners
- ☆ blood pattern analysts (experts who know how blood spatters on objects)
- ☆ entomologists (people who study insects)

CHAPTER 2

GATHERING THE CLUES

↰ Police officers surround a crime scene with yellow tape to keep people from disturbing the evidence.

When the investigation team and Jonathan arrived at the community bicycle center, they entered the building carefully. Everyone knew it was important to step carefully so as not to disturb any possible evidence. Yellow police tape had been put up around portions of the center to keep out people who didn't belong there.

Reading from his notes, Officer Huang explained the situation to the team. "When co-owner Ted Hernandez came in this morning, he noticed broken glass on the sidewalk. The front door was partially open, so he

called the police. We have found that six of the most expensive bicycles are missing, as well as all of the money in the cash register. No paperwork has been taken, and the bikes in for repairs were left behind. There is no physical damage, other than the broken door."

Under Officer Huang's leadership, the team went to work. Jonathan stood back quietly and watched, admiring how everyone knew what to do without being told. Two officers questioned Ted Hernandez, while the police photographer took dozens of pictures.

After the photographer finished her work, Jonathan's father took out his clipboard, graph paper, pencils, compass, and measuring tape. He began to draw. He included the area of the broken glass, measured the hole in the window, and sketched how the glass landed.

Potential evidence is numbered and photographed at a crime scene.

↰ A protractor helps Mr. Elliot measure angles on his diagram.

Mr. Elliot used a protractor and a ruler to draw accurate diagrams. Later, he would make a more precise, detailed drawing. It would include vital information such as the case number, type of crime, names of the team members, and any other identifying information. It would also have a **legend** that explained the meaning of the letters, numbers, and symbols he used in his drawing.

"Jon, let's go outside to see if the officers have found any footprints or other evidence."

Jonathan closed the notebook he was writing in. As he observed the team working, he had taken notes for his report. Just like his father, he was keeping track of the information he might need later.

HIGH-TECH EQUIPMENT

Crime scene team members need a great deal of equipment to do their jobs properly. This includes:

☆ fingerprint equipment (brushes, powders, tape, and a magnifying glass)

☆ casting equipment (plaster of paris, mixing bowls, spatulas, mesh, plastic bags, tongue depressors, modeling clay, and identification tags)

☆ photographic equipment (cameras, lenses, tripod, filters, and memory cards)

☆ evidence packaging supplies (paper bags, metal cans, glass vials, evidence tape, and marking pens)

☆ hand tools (hammers, saws, screwdrivers, wrenches, wire and bolt cutters, shovels, pocket knives, pry bars, and pliers)

☆ other equipment (flashlights, clipboards, chalk, evidence tape, scissors, compass, rope, and electrical cords)

If someone has been injured or killed at the crime scene, the equipment may also include blood collection supplies (sterile cloths, microscope plates, tweezers, and scalpel blades) and a deceased print kit. Some crime scenes may require **biohazard** kits, which include disposable gloves, footwear protectors, face masks, gowns, and waste bags. These items protect the team from dangerous germs, chemicals, or poisons.

11

CHAPTER 3

LEARNING ABOUT THE SCIENTIFIC METHOD

The police make plaster casts of footprints so they can compare them to shoes later on.

Within two hours, all of the evidence had been photographed, drawn, and bagged. Plaster of paris casts had been made of the footprints found at the back of the center.

At the station, the team discussed the break-in.

"Maybe someone was angry with the owners," said an officer.

"Many people don't like the idea that city funds are being used to build and maintain bike trails," said the photographer. "Maybe the person who did this was one of them."

"Before we start discussing motives," interrupted Officer Huang, "let's follow procedure." He walked over to a large whiteboard in a corner of the room.

"Prepare to learn about the scientific method, Jonathan," said Mr. Elliot. "Officer Huang applies it to almost all cases."

Solving a crime requires the help of many different people.

↰ People use the scientific method to help answer questions about the world around them.

"The scientific method is an orderly and organized way of learning and studying our world," said the officer. "We can use it to answer questions we have about science, nature, or just about anything that occurs in our world, including crimes.

"The scientific method is based on our observations, or what we know. Then we develop a possible answer, or **hypothesis**, based on those observations. Once we do that, we can test our hypothesis with experiments or other information we gather.

"Let me show you." Officer Huang picked up a marker and wrote the following on the whiteboard,

THE SCIENTIFIC METHOD
1. Ask a question
2. Gather information and observe/research
3. Make a hypothesis—or guess the answer
4. Experiment to test your hypothesis
5. Analyze your test results
6. Present a conclusion

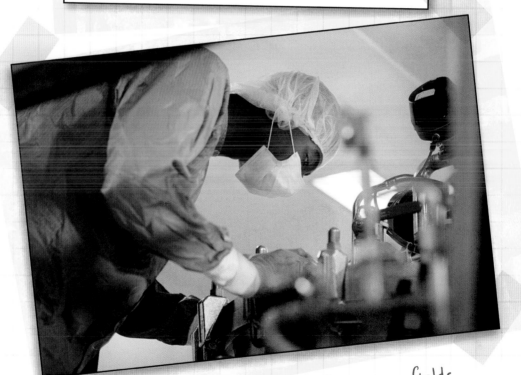

↖ The scientific method is used in many fields, from medical research to crime fighting.

Evidence is carefully documented and studied.

"What question do you think we should ask to solve our crime, Jonathan?" asked Officer Huang.

"I think we should be asking who broke into the bike center."

"Excellent!" said Officer Huang. Then he wrote *Who broke into the bike center?* on the board.

"Now we have to gather information and research. How do we do that?" asked the officer.

"We have to think about all the evidence that was gathered at the crime scene. Then we must decide which evidence might help us, and then study that evidence," said Jonathan.

"Right again," said Officer Huang. "Okay team, let's carefully study

the evidence. We will get the fingerprints tested and see if we can match the shoe print to someone's shoe. Then we will consider various motives for the crime based on what our interviews revealed, and on what was—and was not—taken.

"Remember to be careful and precise as you work. We'll meet tomorrow. Good luck."

Oh no, thought Jonathan. Tomorrow he would be in school. "Don't worry, Jon," whispered Mr. Elliot. "I promise to tell you everything we find out."

Questioning witnesses is an important part of piecing together a case.

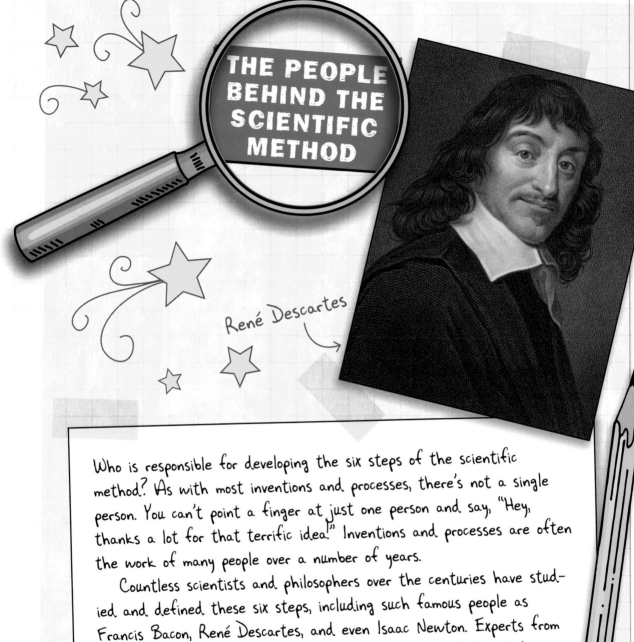

THE PEOPLE BEHIND THE SCIENTIFIC METHOD

René Descartes

Who is responsible for developing the six steps of the scientific method? As with most inventions and processes, there's not a single person. You can't point a finger at just one person and say, "Hey, thanks a lot for that terrific idea!" Inventions and processes are often the work of many people over a number of years.

Countless scientists and philosophers over the centuries have studied and defined these six steps, including such famous people as Francis Bacon, René Descartes, and even Isaac Newton. Experts from many fields have done experiments, written papers, and debated ways to improve the process. In fact, scientists are still trying to refine the scientific process to see if they can come up with an even better process for understanding our world.

CHAPTER 4

APPLYING ADDITIONAL STEPS

Jonathan was excited when his dad's car finally pulled into the driveway.

The next day, Jonathan looked out of the living room window yet again, letting out a sigh. He felt like he would explode with curiosity by the time his father finally came home from work. He could not wait to hear what the team had learned from the evidence. Had they found out enough to move to the next step and make a hypothesis—or guess who might have committed the crime?

"Well?" Jonathan asked his father, when he finally got home from work.

"Well, what?" asked Mr. Elliot innocently, but his grin gave him away. He knew Jonathan would be eager to hear about the investigation.

"We did not find out anything from the fingerprints, so that means the person probably has not been arrested before," explained Jonathan's father. "We identified what kind of shoe the **intruder** was wearing, but it's a common brand so that wasn't very helpful."

Jonathan sat back in his chair, disappointed. "So, no hypothesis yet?"

Some crimes can be solved by matching a shoe print to a shoe.

Investigators can use special dust to reveal a fingerprint on a surface.

Mr. Elliot chuckled as his son sat forward eagerly. "We've come up with some ideas. Our first hypothesis was that the break-in was committed by a group of local people who have been protesting the use of city funds for bike trails." Jonathan nodded. He remembered that idea coming up the day before.

"So we studied the evidence for what it could tell us. While the fingerprints and shoe prints didn't help us prove or disprove that hypothesis, other details did," his father continued. "First, the store was not damaged, so this was not a revenge crime. The intruders were not angry. Second, we talked to the head of the group we suspected, and he said they were meeting at the library when the crime most likely occurred."

Someone might have stolen the bikes to make money by selling them illegally.

"The evidence definitely did not support your first hypothesis then. What did you do next, Dad?"

"We kept gathering evidence, like the scientific method says to do," replied Mr. Elliot. "Only the most expensive bikes and the cash were taken. The cheaper bikes and those needing repair were left behind. This leads us to hypothesize that . . . " He paused.

" . . . that the person who did this was looking for some quick cash, rather than taking revenge or stealing for a personal reason," added Jonathan.

"Exactly," agreed Mr. Elliot. "The center's owners said when we interviewed them that a couple of new volunteers joined the previous

morning. They showed a great deal of interest in the value of each of the bikes."

"Now you had to test your hypothesis to see if it was correct," said Jonathan excitedly.

"Exactly! All volunteers have to fill out papers that include their names and addresses. Officer Huang examined the papers and went to the address the new volunteers gave. It was a fake address. Just an abandoned building."

Jonathan sat back, frustrated. "But," added Mr. Elliot with a dramatic pause, "we asked around the neighborhood and have a lead on where the men might be living. We will find out tomorrow."

The police gained the information they needed by talking to people in the neighborhood.

"What happens if you find them?" asked Jonathan.

"Just like the scientific method says," reminded his father, "we will experiment to see if our hypothesis is correct. We will fingerprint them and take a look at their shoes. We'll see if they have **alibis** for the time of the crime. And then we will—"

"—analyze the test results!" the two said at the same time.

When Jonathan went to bed that night, his mind was filled with possibilities of what the police might find and how the scientific method was applied. This had definitely turned into the most interesting home-work assignment of the year.

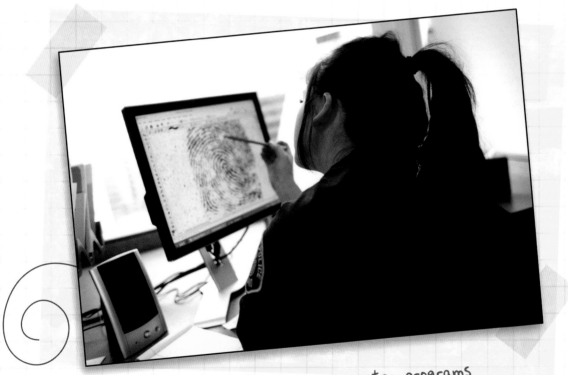

Police officers use computer programs to compare fingerprints.

PLEASE TRY THIS AT HOME

Would you like to learn the basics of being a sketch preparer like Jonathan's father? You can see if you have a talent for the job by creating your own diagrams. Start by choosing a place to draw. It could be your backyard, a room in your house, a spot in the park, or a porch at a friend's house. While you're at it, think about a question that your drawing might help answer. Who left footprints in the lawn? How did the family dog manage to reach a pie on the counter?

Once you've chosen your location, it's time to start drawing. Make sure you have a large piece of paper, plenty of sharp pencils, and a good eraser. Draw everything according to **scale**, and include points of reference. As you draw, include signs, sidewalks, buildings, and roads if you are outside, and furnishings, rooms, and walls if you are inside. Include any people if they are part of the scene.

You will need to take accurate measurements to include in the drawings, so take along a tape measure or ruler. (Some of today's sketchers use laser measuring tools and survey equipment. The sketches are analyzed on computers.) Include a legend to identify what you have labeled in your drawing.

CHAPTER 5

SOLVING THE PUZZLE

Jonathan had enjoyed working on a case with his dad.

A few days later, Jonathan was sitting in class when his teacher called his name.

"Jonathan, please stay after class for a moment," said Mrs. Coffman.

Jonathan waited by the teacher's desk as the other students filed out.

"I read your report about going to work with your father, Jon. It was extremely interesting. He has a fascinating job.

"You did a great job with your report. Did they ever solve the mystery of the bike store break-in?"

"They sure did, by following the scientific method, too. They used the fifth step—analyzing test results—when they located the two men and matched their fingerprints to the ones found at the crime scene. They also matched the footprints to those left in the dirt around the back of the bike center," Jonathan explained.

Mrs. Coffman was eager to hear whether the bike theft case was solved.

"Finally, they presented a conclusion that the two new volunteers were the men who committed the crime. That conclusion was proven correct when the men confessed."

"I'm glad the police were able to solve the case," said Mrs. Coffman. "You certainly learned a great deal about police work and the scientific method with this assignment."

"Absolutely," agreed Jonathan. "I'm already planning to use the method to help me make decisions now. In fact," he added with a chuckle, "I may even apply the steps to what to have for lunch today."

"Well, remember it is only cafeteria food. Don't analyze the results too closely," replied Mrs. Coffman with a smile.

Sometimes people confess to a crime they committed once they see the evidence against them.

THE SCIENTIFIC METHOD IN DAILY LIFE

Even though the scientific method may sound like it applies only to questions about science, the six steps can frequently be used to help you make some of the decisions in your daily life. For example, you could apply the method to learn where you lost your wallet.

1. Ask a question: Where did I lose my wallet?
2. Gather information and observe or research: I went shopping with Mom this afternoon. When I returned home, I noticed my wallet was missing.
3. Make a hypothesis: I lost my wallet while we were in the supermarket.
4. Experiment to test your hypothesis: I searched all over the house, but could not find my wallet. I looked in all my jacket and pants pockets, and it wasn't in any of those places. I went back to the supermarket with Mom to ask if someone there had found it. The manager said someone had found my wallet and had given it to him. He gave my wallet back to me.
5. Analyze your test results: I found my wallet after testing my hypothesis with experiments.
6. Present a conclusion: I lost my wallet in the supermarket and someone found it and gave it to the store manager.

GLOSSARY

alibis (AL-uh-byez) claims that a person accused of a crime was somewhere else when the crime was committed

biohazard (BYE-oh-haz-urd) a health risk posed by the possible release of a serious germ or disease into the environment

chain of custody (CHAYN uhv KUHS-tuh-dee) the movement and location of physical evidence from the time it is obtained until it is presented in court

hypothesis (hye-PAH-thi-sis) an idea that could explain how something works but must be proven by the scientific method

impression evidence (im-PRESH-uhn EV-i-duhns) any object or material that takes on the form of another object through physical contact, such as fingerprints

intruder (in-TROO-duhr) someone who goes into a place where he or she is not wanted

legend (LEJ-uhnd) the words written beneath or beside a map or drawing to explain the meaning of symbols used in the drawing

scale (SKALE) the ratio between the measurements on a drawing or map

surveyors (sur-VAY-uhrz) someone who measures the lines and angles of a piece of land to make a map or plan

FOR MORE INFORMATION

BOOKS

Cameron, Schyrlet. *Scientific Method Investigation: A Step-by-Step Guide for Middle-School Students.* Quincy, IL: Mark Twain Media, 2010.

MacLeod, Elizabeth. *Bones Never Lie: How Forensics Helps Solve History's Mysteries.* Toronto, Ontario, Canada: Annick Press, 2013.

Mooney, Carla. *Forensics: Uncover the Science and Technology of Crime Scene Investigation.* White River Junction, VT: Nomad Press, 2013.

WEB SITES

Forensics for Kids

www.forensicscience.org/resources/forensics-for-kids

Visit this page for links to a lot of different Web sites about the science of crime solving.

Public Broadcasting Service (PBS) — Forensics and Investigations

www.pbs.org/topics/science-nature/forensics-investigations

Watch videos and read articles about new and creative ways people are solving mysteries.

Science in Action—Scientific Method for Kids

www.science-fair-projects-and-more.com/scientific-method-for-kids.html

Find out more about the scientific method and how it works.

INDEX

ABOUT THE AUTHOR

Tamra Orr is an author living in the Pacific Northwest. Orr has a degree in Secondary Education and English from Ball State University. She is the mother to four, and the author of more than 350 books for readers of all ages. When she isn't writing or reading books, she is writing letters to friends all over the world. Although fascinated by all aspects of science, most of her current scientific method skills are put to use tracking down lost socks, missing keys, and overdue library books.